DUCTIGAMI

The Art of the Tape

DUCTIGAMI

The Art of the Tape

JOE WILSON

The BOSTON MILLS PRESS

A Boston Mills Press Book

Sixth printing, 2011

Library and Archives Canada Cataloguing in Publication

Wilson, Joe, 1962-
Ductigami : the art of the tape / Joe Wilson. -- Rev. ed.
ISBN-13: 978-1-55046-429-0
ISBN-10: 1-55046-429-9
1. Duct tape--Humor. 2. Wit and humor (English). I. Title.
PN6231.D79W54 2006   C818'.5402   C2006-902791-9

Publisher Cataloging-in-Publication Data (U.S.)

Wilson, Joe, 1962-
Ductigami : the art of the tape / Joe Wilson.
Rev. ed.
[96] p. : ill. (some col.) ;   cm.
Summary: A funny and useful book with
18 duct tape projects.
ISBN-13: 978-1-55046-429-0
ISBN-10: 1-55046-429-9
1. Handicraft. 2. Duct tape -- Humor. I. Title.
745.5 dc22   TT157.W576 2006

Published by
Boston Mills Press, 2006
132 Main Street, Erin, Ontario
N0B 1T0
Tel 519-833-2407
Fax 519-833-2195

In Canada:
Distributed by Firefly Books Ltd.
66 Leek Crescent
Richmond Hill, Ontario,
Canada L4B 1H1

In the United States:
Distributed by Firefly Books (U.S.) Inc.
P.O. Box 1338, Ellicott Station
Buffalo, New York 14205

The publisher gratefully acknowledges the financial support
for our publishing program by the Government of Canada
through the Book Publishing Industry Development Program.

Design by Darrach Design
Additional design by McCorkindale Advertising & Design
Cover design by Gillian Stead

Printed in China

Many thanks to
Wendy Duncan, Rick Haufe, Ritchie Overland,
and Red Green (just because).

This book is dedicated
to those who know duct tape,
to those who do but say they don't,
to those who don't but should,
and those who should know it but don't.

Have I left anyone out?

Oh, and my mom because she's neat.

Contents

Introduction

Congratulations, you now hold in your hands *Ductigami: The Art of the Tape*, a book that reveals the essential techniques of duct-tape-folding to create objects of transcendence, wonder and inspired usefulness.

Not to be confused with origami, the ancient Japanese art of paper-folding to create delicate, fragile items for the moment, ductigami employs ordinary off-the-shelf duct tape in the creation of functional folded objects that are built to suffer the rigors of modern life. Can a majestic origami crane withstand an assault with a water pistol? Can an origami jack-in-the-box survive a three-year-old? We think not.

Once you master the art of the tape, you will be able to construct some of the world's most unique items of function and fashion. And part of their beauty is that if they ever wear out, they can be repaired quickly with more duct tape.

Ductigamists hold the future in their sticky-fingered hands. Master tapers know that as the new millennium approaches and world economies boom and bust, they will always have a marketable craft.

Ductigami is more challenging than a crossword puzzle, more useful than a welder's certificate, more durable than a Duracell, more invigorating than Viagra (when used correctly), and as long as you have tape, you'll never be caught short of a gift for any occasion.

No doubt you're anxious to get started.

Let's roll the tape.

The Role of the Roll: A Ripping History

During the Second World War, the United States military put out a tender for the development of a strong mending material. This material had to be waterproof and tearable by hand so that soldiers could use it on the battlefield.

A division of Johnson and Johnson Co. rose to the challenge and developed an olive-drab "military tape," a cloth-mesh tape covered in a rubber-based waterproof adhesive.

This tape was first used to keep ammunition boxes dry, but it was soon discovered that this military tape could be employed to make quick repairs to Jeeps and all sorts of other military equipment. Foot soldiers called the tape "gun tape." The air force used it to cover gun ports on the wings of planes, thus reducing drag during takeoff. (As a bonus, pilots could tell if a gun had malfunctioned, as a faulty gun would still be covered in unbroken tape after firing.)

After the war, a housing boom commenced in the United States. Many of these new homes featured forced-air furnaces and air-conditioning, both of which relied on ductwork to move air throughout the living spaces. Though a variety of products were tried in an effort to find the best connective material for these ducts, Johnson and Johnson military tape proved superior. The color was changed from olive drab to sheet-metal gray, and that's how duct tape as we know it was born.

This magical, pliable, metal-like fastener can hold almost anything together. Red Green calls it the handyman's secret weapon. NASCAR claims it's the 200-mile-per-hour tape. The U.S. Air Force ups the ante, calling it the 1,000-mile-per-hour tape. NASA actually has a policy stating that every space shuttle mission must carry at least one roll of "the gray tape" on board. Remember *Apollo 13* ("Houston, we have a problem")? They used duct tape to bring those astronauts home!

Ductigami Frequently Asked Questions

Q: Is ductigami hard to do?

A: Your first hands-on attempt will feel awkward. Very few people have tried to cut, fold and seam this tape. You have probably only torn it into short, sticky strips for domestic patching jobs. But once you get started, you'll discover that ductigami is actually very easy to do.

Q: Does duct tape only come in gray?

A: No! A number of companies produce different colors of tape. One company sells over a dozen different colors. There's classic gray, but also black, white, brown, yellow, red, blue, purple, kelly green, olive green, orange, gold...

Q: There are several brands of duct tape on the market and a range of prices. What's the difference?

A: The main difference between low-end and high-end duct tape is the number of threads in the cloth mesh. Remember, duct tape is a cloth mesh covered with a waterproof rubber-based adhesive. If you rip off a piece of tape and look at it closely, you can actually count the number of threads. These threads are called the "scrim." The more threads per inch, the stronger the tape. The stronger the tape, the more costly it is to produce. "Military tape" has a 40-pound rip strength. Less expensive tapes have only a 20-pound rip strength. Generally, the more you spend on tape, the less tape you have to use.

Q: Is there a project I should attempt first?

A: The most important thing is to get a feel for the tape. Most projects in this book require you to manipulate the tape in slightly different ways. You should try to master the basics first. The phone-book cover on page 35 is a good project to begin with (because it's simple and everyone should have one). Or the wallet on page 21 (because it's cool).

Q: What do I do if the tape sticks to my fingers?

A: It's tape; it's sticky. You'll get a feel for it. Ductigami mastery is a journey of patience — and something worth getting wrapped up in.

Q: What do I do if the tape shifts sideways and leaves a mark on the piece beneath it?

A: This is what I call "adhesive migration." The unsightly residue can be removed by rubbing it off with your thumb or fingers.

Q: Have you considered a ductigami underwear project?

A: Ouch.

Ductigami Basics

There are four basic steps to creating ductigami objects. Spend some time learning these basic patterns and you'll spend far less time freeing yourself from sticky entanglements and creating projects on par with Aunt Doris's first ceramic ashtray.

Keep in mind that the measurements provided here are finished measurements. Always make your pieces a bit oversized and trim them to the appropriate size. Do your cutting on a cutting board, not on the dining-room table or the top of a 1910 Steinway grand piano.

STEP 1   The Sheet

Just as a sheet of paper is used to create origami, a sheet of duct tape is used to create ductigami. Unfortunately, sheets of paper are easy to come by, sheets of duct tape must be made from scratch by the ductigamist. The good news is that no trees are harmed in the creation of ductigami objects.

1 On your work area, cut 7 or 8 strips of tape just longer than the pattern requires. For instance, a wallet uses strips approximately 8 1/2 inches long (22 cm). This is the finished measurement. Make the strips slightly longer and trim them to the proper size.

2 Lay a piece of tape on your work area, sticky side up. We'll call this piece A.

3 Lay a second piece of tape (piece B), sticky side down, horizontally halfway across piece A.

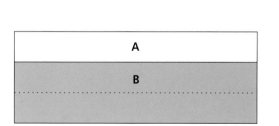

4 Fold the exposed sticky side of piece A over to cover half of piece B, with its dry side up.

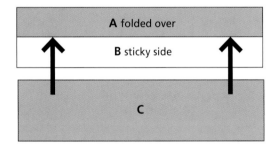

5 You have just produced one sealed side of your sheet. Now for the fun part. Grip one end of the tape strips on your work surface. Rip them off of the surface and flip them over. Grip, rip and flip.

6 Place your third strip of tape with its sticky side down to cover the sticky side up of piece B.

You should end up with the strip once again placed on your work surface with a sticky half-width of tape exposed along its horizontal edge.

7 Once again, grip, rip and flip the entire length of tape.

8 Repeat this process until you have used all your pieces of tape.

9 When you get to your last piece, fold the final sticky edge over onto the dry edge beside it, as you did in step 3.

10 You should end up with a ductigamiable sheet of tape with no sticky edges. Simply trim the sheet to the size you require for your project and commence ductigamiing.

1 Cut five pieces of tape 7 1/2 inches long (19 cm) and make a sheet of tape (as described on previous pages).

2 Cut another five pieces of tape 7 1/2 inches long (19 cm) and make another sheet of tape.

3 Cut your two sheets in half so that you have four pieces about 3 3/4 inches wide (9.5 cm).

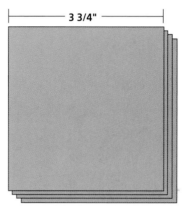

4 Fold two of the pieces so that there is a 1/8-inch (.5 cm) space overlap at the top of each. Line the two folded pieces up one on top of the other, again leaving a 1/8-inch (.5 cm) space between the two pieces.

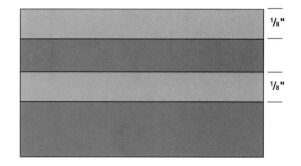

5 When aligned, flip the two pieces over and tape them together.

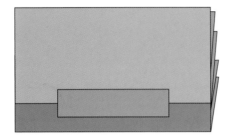

6 Open the section between the two pieces you just taped together and place a small piece of tape along the bottom to create a duct-tape seam. (This will insure that items placed in the slots don't stick.)

7 Repeat this process with the remaining two pieces to create two sets of slots.

The number of slots you need to make will depend on your project.

STEP 3   Strips

The Little Strip

1 Take a piece of tape, whatever size the pattern calls for, and fold it lengthwise. Use a ruler and sharp knife to trim off any overlapping sticky parts. Or you can take the same piece of tape and fold both sides back toward the center until they overlap slightly, thus avoiding any sticky parts.

The Big Strip

1 Cut two pieces to the length required for your project and lay one strip, sticky side up, on your work area.

2 Take the remaining piece and lay it sticky face to sticky face halfway up the first piece.

3 Fold the exposed sticky part over. Grip, rip and flip, and do the same with the other side.

Fold **A** over **B**

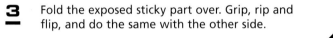

Fold **B** over **A**

4 Trim to the size you need. For a belt or other heavy-duty item, use a big strip and cover it with two or more pieces to thicken it up.

STEP 4   Loops

You can make your loop strip small or large, whatever your pattern calls for, or as dictated by the width of your belt.

1 Make a strip of the approximate size necessary. Connect the ends so that you end up with a loop and seal the ends together with another piece of tape both on the inside and on the outside. This sort of loop can be attached to whatever you're making to allow a belt to pass through it. Make as many as you need for your project.

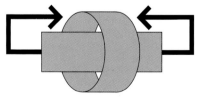

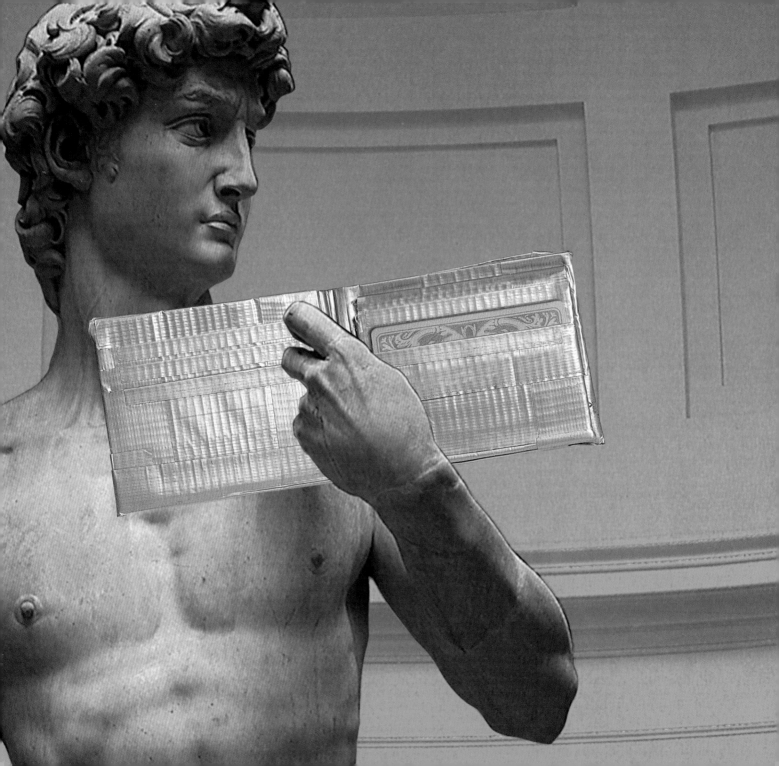

Wallet

You've seen them. You've read about them. Now you're ready to make your very own duct-tape wallet! The 100-percent waterproof wallet! Rumor has it that they float. A lady came up to me recently at a trade show and told me that when her husband fell into a lake, his duct-tape wallet floated to the surface. He sank. She had a look on her face. I think she pushed him.

1 Create one sheet of tape 8 1/4 by 6 3/4 inches (21 x 17 cm) (approximately 8 strips) and two sets of card slots.

2 Fold your sheet almost in half, leaving 1/8-inch (.5 cm) at the top. (Look at your present wallet. It should look like that.)

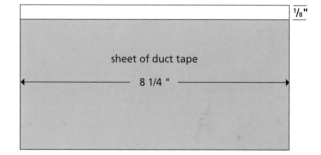

sheet of duct tape

8 1/4 "

1/8"

3 Take your folded sheet and lay one credit card pocket along one side. Cut a piece of tape about 4 inches (10 cm) long and lay it on top with 1/2-inch (1 cm) covering the card pockets.

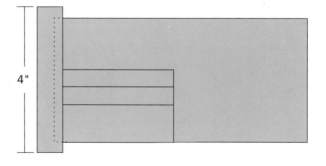

4"

4 Turn the wallet over. Cut the exposed tape strip at the two points illustrated and fold the sticky pieces over into the inside of the wallet at the top and over onto the back first. Then turn the wallet over and fold the remaining piece over and tuck accordingly.

5 Lay the second credit card pocket on the other side and repeat steps 3 and 4.

6 Cut a piece of tape 4 inches long (10 cm) and lay it down the middle of the wallet so that both credit card pockets are covered. Now fold the top sticky piece into the inside of the wallet's main pocket and the bottom sticky piece onto the back.

7 Cut a piece of tape 9 1/2 inches long (24 cm) and lay it across the bottom 3/4-inch (2 cm) of the wallet.

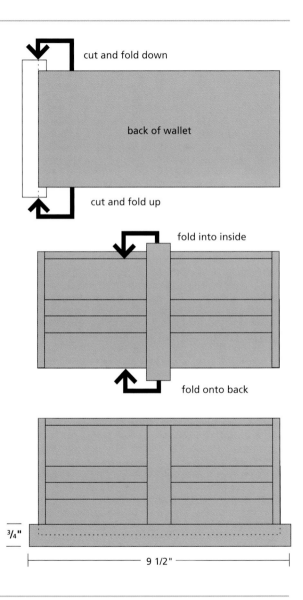

cut and fold down

back of wallet

cut and fold up

fold into inside

fold onto back

3/4"

9 1/2"

8 Turn the wallet over. Cut the exposed tape strip at the two points illustrated and fold the sticky pieces over onto the body of the wallet.

9 You're almost done. Simply cut at the points marked.

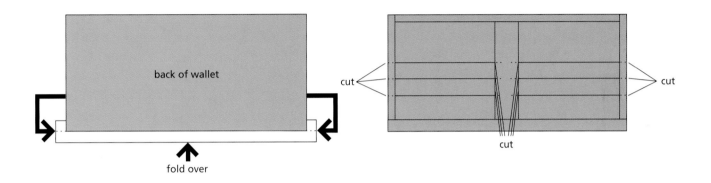

Extra Stuff: Bill Divider, Hidden Pocket, Pull-out ID Holder.

These have to be made before you assemble your wallet.

Bill Divider

1 Make a sheet of tape the same length as your wallet and about 3 1/8 inches (8 cm) high (so that it fits inside and still allows 1/8-inch (.5 cm) at the top. Place this sheet inside your wallet. Line it up along the crease that will be the bottom of your wallet. Tape it into place so that it doesn't move when you assemble your wallet.

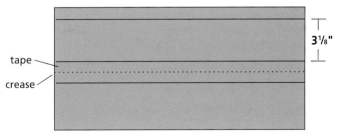

2 Fold your sheet over at the 2 3/4-inch (7 cm) mark and trim off the top as illustrated.

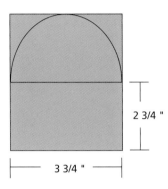

2 3/4 "

3 3/4 "

3 Make a set of credit card slots and install them as illustrated. Adjust them to fit. Because you're using a smaller area, the distance between the slots will be shorter.

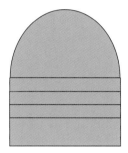

4 Tape the sides and bottom.

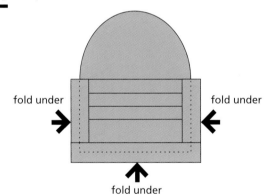

fold under

fold under

fold under

5 To create the part that keeps this holder closed, make a little strip that is 3 3/4 inches (9.5 cm) long. Fold under and tape it down.

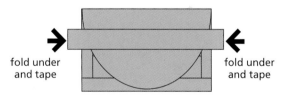

fold under
and tape

fold under
and tape

6 This pull-out holder should tuck into the top credit card slot of your wallet. Open the holder and tuck the top flap into the top credit card slot on your wallet.

Waterproof-Flakproof Apron

Yes, this apron is waterproof. And, yes, real men do dishes. The "flakproof" part works like this: If you put on the apron and do the dishes, you're going to get a whole lot less flak. Peace in our time. Once again duct tape has a strategic military use.

1 Create one sheet 26 by 32 inches (66 x 81 cm), approximately 40 pieces.

2 Create three big strips: one 26 inches long (66 cm) (for the neck), one 24 inches long (61 cm) and one 13 inches long (33 cm) (for the belt).

3 Positioning your sheet vertically, mark off and cut a 7-inch (18 cm) square from each side of the top of your sheet. (You can attach these squares as pockets on the front of your apron.) The top of your apron will now measure 12 inches (31 cm).

4 Attach your 26-inch (66 cm) big strip at each side of the 12-inch (31 cm) top. Tape it down firmly on the back of the apron (about 2 inches [5 cm] of tape) so that it can be hung around your neck.

5 Make marks 24 inches (66 cm) up from the bottom of your sheet on each side. Take your other two big strips and tape them to the sides of the apron along the 24-inch (66 cm) marks. This is your belt. You can obtain a plastic claspable belt buckle at most sports stores.

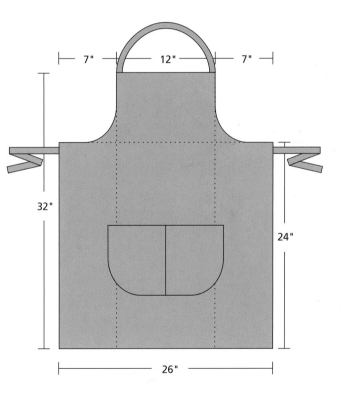

Beverage Holders

Pop Can Holder

If the heat from your hand is about 98.6 degrees Fahrenheit (37°C), how long can your cold one stay cold? Your hand heats your drink faster than the air, even on a hot day. A duct-tape pop can holder helps keep pop colder longer because the palm of your hand never touches the can. (Say that three times fast.)

1 Create two big strips 8 7/8 inches (22.5 cm) each (the top and bottom) and one small strip 4 3/4 inches (12 cm) (the cradle).

2 Now create the piece that holds it all together. Cut three strips of tape 9 1/2 inches long (24 cm). Lay the first piece (A) sticky side up on your work area. Lay the second piece (B) sticky side down halfway horizontally up the first piece. Fold A over B.

3 Grip, rip and flip. Turn the piece over so that the sticky side is exposed. Place the remaining single piece (C) sticky side down on the exposed sticky length of piece B.

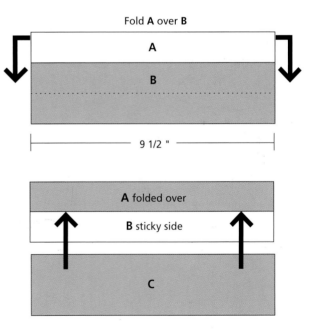

4 Fold piece A over B (dry side to dry side) and then fold the sticky part of piece C over to cover them. You should end up with a thick piece of tape about 9 1/2 inches long (24 cm) and about 1-inch wide (2.5 cm). This is the handle.

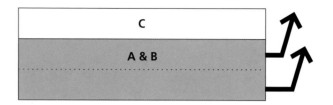

5 Take one 8 7/8-inch (22.5 cm) piece and loop it to form a circle, then tape the ends together on both inside and outside seams. This is the top.

6 Do the same with the other 8 7/8-inch (22.5 cm) piece. This is the bottom.

7 Add the 4 3/4-inch (12 cm) piece to the inside of this circle to act as the cradle that will hold your pop can at the bottom.

8 Now take your 9 1/2-inch (24 cm) piece, the handle, and fold it in half. Slide your holder into the top of the fold (the closed part) and tape it into place on both the inside and outside of the circle.

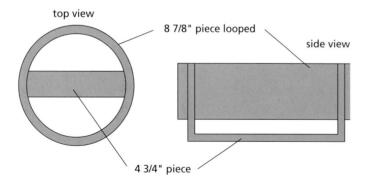

top view

8 7/8" piece looped

side view

4 3/4" piece

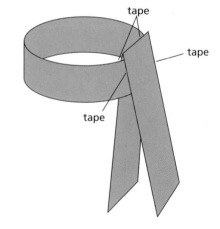

tape

tape

tape

9 Next, tape the open end of the handle to the outside bottom of your holder.

Remember: reinforce, reinforce, reinforce!

To load, put the top on first, then slide on the bottom. The same goes for the Beer Bottle Holder below.

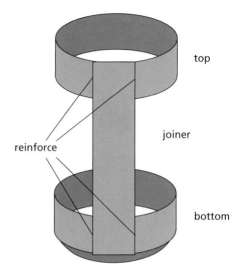

top

joiner

reinforce

bottom

Beer Bottle Holder

Again, this will help to keep your fermented barley-based beverage cool. You're a warm-blooded mammal. Your hands radiate more heat than a catcher's mitt in a mid-August no-hitter. If you're thinking, "Hey, buddy, my beer doesn't spend enough time in the bottle to get warm!" Let me just say that they have regular support meetings for people like you, with comfortable folding chairs and only the occasional hymn. Enjoy!

1 Create one little strip 4 3/4 inches (12 cm) long (the cradle), one big strip 5 5/8 inches (13.5 cm) long for the top, one big strip 8 1/16 inches (21.5 cm) long for the bottom, and a handle 14 1/4 inches (36 cm).

2 Assemble as in Pop Can Holder above.

Note: When you attach the handle to this one, tape the piece of the handle that covers the top piece down. The opening for your hand will start under the top piece.

Coffee Cup Holder

This unit will help you get a safe handle on your morning coffee. It can be custom-designed to fit any cup. Get an empty take-out cup in the size of your preference and build your holder around it. You'll notice that the top is larger than the bottom. That's why, unlike with the pop can holder, you don't have to construct a cradle on the bottom to keep the cup from slipping through. It's a gravity thing.

1 For your average large take-out cup, create two big strips, one 10 1/16 inches (25.5 cm) (top side piece) and one 8 1/16 (21.5 cm) (bottom side piece), then one strip 9 1/16 inches (23 cm) (the handle).

2 Take the 10 1/16-inch (25.5 cm) piece and loop it to form a circle, then tape the ends together on both inside and outside seams. This is the top side piece.

3 Do the same with the 8 1/16-inch (20.5 cm) piece. This is the bottom side piece.

4 Now take your 9 1/16-inch (23 cm) piece, the handle, and fold it in half. Slide your holder into the top of the fold (the closed part) and tape it into place on both the inside and outside of the circle.

5 Next, tape the open end of the handle to the outside bottom ring of your holder. Tape a piece along the length of the handle so that it covers the top before you fold the handle over. This will provide extra support.

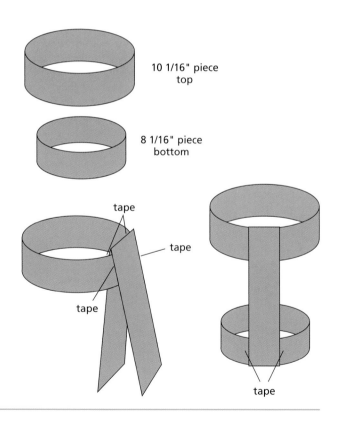

10 1/16" piece top

8 1/16" piece bottom

tape

tape

tape

tape

tape

Disclaimer: The most important part of the construction of any coffee-cup holder is to reinforce the top and bottom pieces where they join the handle. Remember that coffee is hot and that duct tape has an adhesive base. When the tape warms up, it will have a tendency to separate unless it is properly reinforced. Take time to do this. Simple math states that Hot Coffee + Lap = Yikes!

Water Bottle Holder

Make this holder to the size of the water bottle you plan to hold.

1 You will need to create two big strips 24 inches (61 cm) long for the shoulder strap, three more big strips measuring the circumference of your bottle, and a small strip that will go across the cradle of your holder to keep the bottle from dropping out.

2 Measure your bottle and make your three big strips.

3 Make loops from your three big strips, the same as in the Pop Can Holder.

4 Attach the little strip to the inside of the bottom loop so that it acts as the cradle that will keep your water bottle from falling out.

5 Take your 2-by-24-inch (5 x 61 cm) big strips and join them together. Starting at the bottom, attach them to the big loops.

Once everything is taped in place and reinforced, you will have a very cool water bottle holder.

You can do a variation on the shoulder strap. If you make it longer and attach it to the top big strip, you can use a plastic buckle to make a belt, so that it can be worn around the waist or strapped to a golf bag.

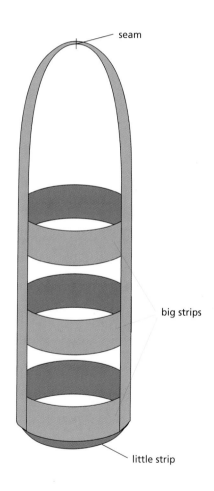

seam

big strips

little strip

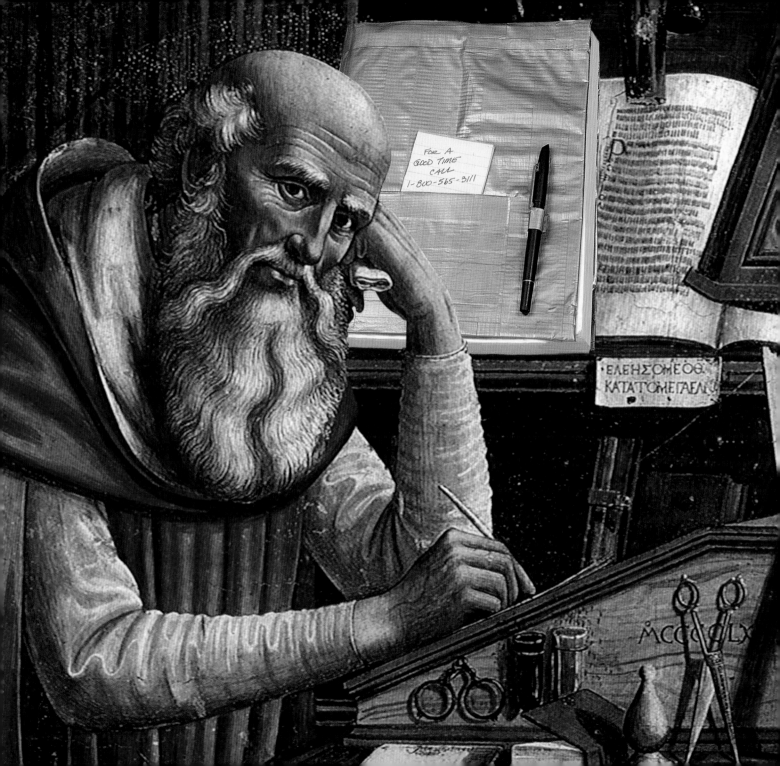

Phone Book Cover

You can make a cover for any book you desire once you figure out the secret mathematical formula I employ. I chose the phone book as a project because a) most people have a phone book even if they own no other books, and b) well before I receive my new phone book, my old phone book always looks like it has been used as nesting material by a family of lab mice.

Before you start, haul out the phone book that you're making the cover for.

1 Measure the width of your phone book. Most are about 9 1/16 inches (23 cm) wide.

2 Measure the spine width of the book. This will vary, depending on where you live.

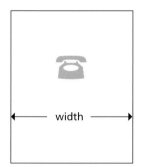

3 Measure the height of the book. Most are about 11 inches (28 cm).

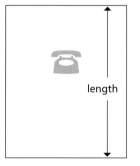

4 Now here's the tricky math part. Add the width of the book x 2 + the spine width + an additional 7 7/8 inches (20 cm). This equals the length of sheet of tape you need to create.

5 Create a sheet using the height measurement of the book by the width measurement that you just figured out. Cover any rough outside edges with tape.

6 Measure 4 inches (10 cm) in from each end of the long sheet and fold the ends in at this point and tape them down.

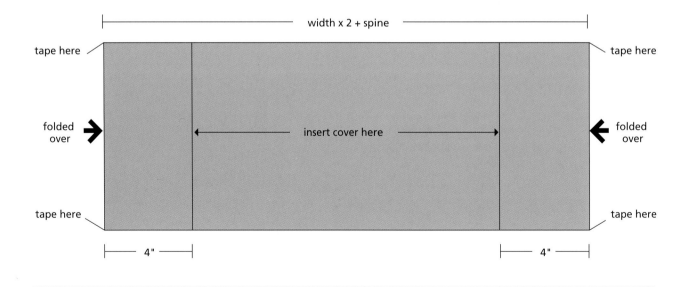

width x 2 + spine

tape here

tape here

folded over

insert cover here

folded over

tape here

tape here

4"

4"

7 Try it on for size. Make sure that the cover fits not only when the book is open but also when it is closed.

8 You can add extra touches if you so desire. Add slots (as many as you like) to hold business cards with important phone numbers (that we write on the back of those business cards).

inside front cover

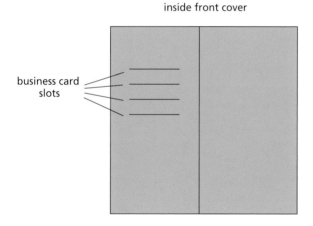

business card slots

9 On the front of the book, you can make a pocket to hold a pad of paper for message-taking. Create a small sheet of tape 4 inches by 5 1/8 inches (10 cm x 13 cm) and tape it into place on the sides and bottom. Next, make a small strip about 3 1/8 inches (8 cm) long and tape it into place beside the pocket to create a pen holder.

front cover

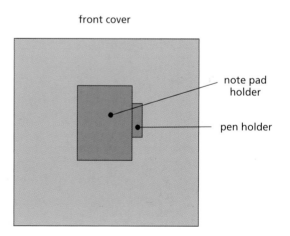

note pad holder

pen holder

Cooler/Lunchbox

Hey, anything that keeps you from losing your lunch is a good thing. If it's waterproof and holds ice, that's even better. Oh, sure, you could go out and buy a nice lunchbox with a popular cartoon character or a company logo on it, but those will turn out to be worth big money if you hang onto them for a few decades and don't use them. Why buy a cooler that later you're going to wish you hadn't used? Why put that kind of stress in your life? Buy the G.I. Jane Meets Barbie lunchbox, put it in your attic and get busy with the duct tape.

1 Create a 35-by-9-inch (89 x 23 cm) sheet, two 7-by-7-inch (18 x 18 cm) sheets, one 11-inch (28 cm) little strip, and two big strips (to be used as a shoulder strap).

2 Once you've made your sheets, go over them with even more tape to thicken them up. This will give the box extra support and greater insulation. Did you know that the R-value of doubled duct tape is 3.679, equal to that of Silly Putty? OK, maybe not. We made that part up.

3 Fold and crease your large sheet into five 7-inch (18 cm) sections.

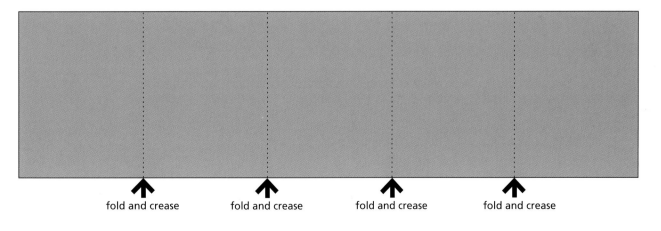

fold and crease   fold and crease   fold and crease   fold and crease

4 Add your two other 7-inch (18 cm) sections to what will be the bottom of your cooler/lunchbox and tape them to the larger sheet to create sides.

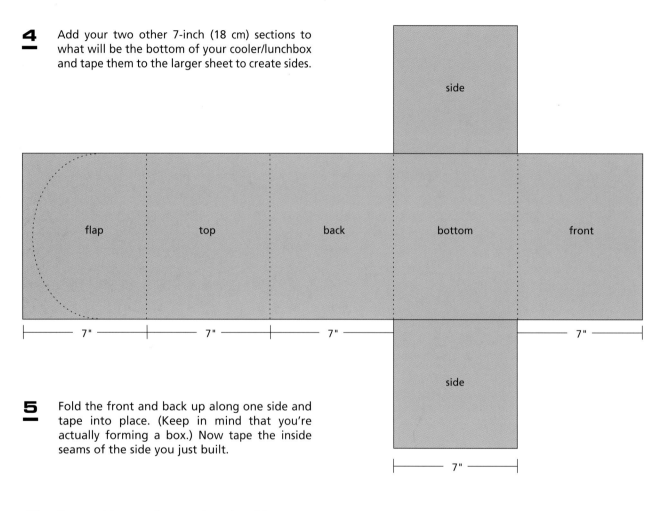

flap

top

back

bottom

front

side

side

7"   7"   7"   7"

7"

5 Fold the front and back up along one side and tape into place. (Keep in mind that you're actually forming a box.) Now tape the inside seams of the side you just built.

6 Repeat this procedure on the other side.

7 Once the box is built, fold the top down. (You may want to add an extra strip on each side of the top to create a better fit.)

8 Measure where you would like the box's closing flap to go. Take your 11-inch (28 cm) strip and attach it across the front of the box to secure the flap. Cut to round off the flap so that it slides easily in and out of the strip on the front of the box.

9 Take your two big strips and tape them up from the bottom of the box, connecting them at the top with additional tape. This becomes your shoulder strap.

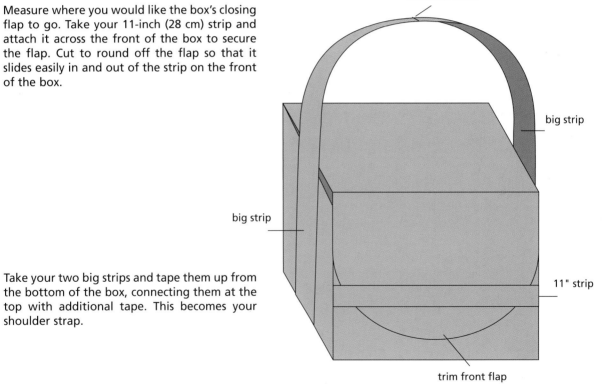

reinforce seam

big strip

big strip

11" strip

trim front flap

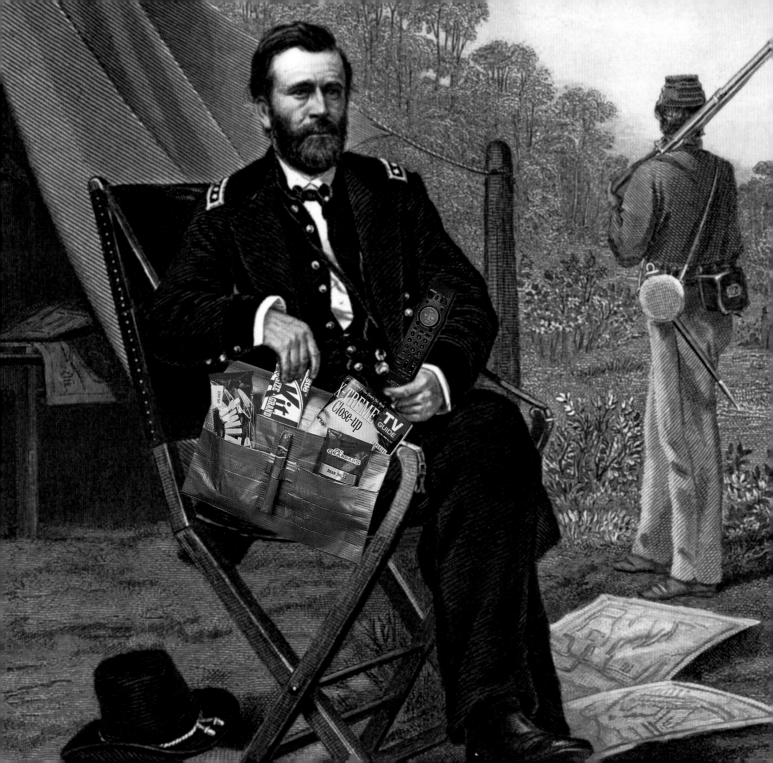

TV Chair Caddy

Have you ever lost the remote control? I mean, really experienced the gnawing, blinding, sweat-producing terror of realizing you've lost the remote control after you've already kicked back in your favorite TV chair and balanced your drink on the arm and your snacks on your chest? Well, fear no more. This multi-pocketed TV Chair Caddy will help you keep all of your TV essentials together in one place — *your* place.

1 Create one 36-by-13-inch (91 x 33 cm) sheet and four 5-by-6 1/2-inch (13 x 16.5 cm) sheets. The small sheets will be for the pockets in your caddy.

2 Take your large sheet and fold it back toward the center 7 inches (18 cm). Tape along the sides to form a pocket for *TV Guides*, crossword puzzles, etc.

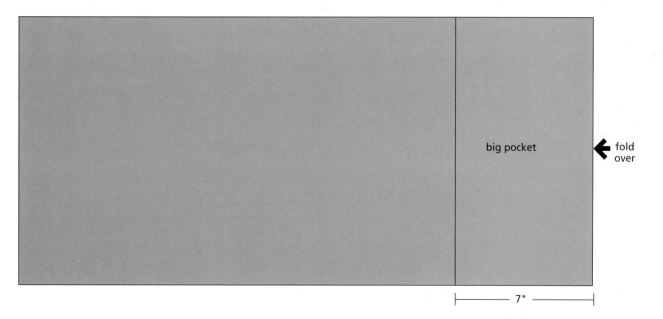

big pocket

← fold over

⊢——— 7" ———⊣

3 Take two of the small pocket sheets and place them on top of the pocket that you just made. Tape them into place to create two smaller pockets for remote controls.

4 Optional: If you make a little strip, bow it into a V shape and tape it into place between the two pockets, you will have a place to clip a pen. Make it bigger to accommodate a cigar.

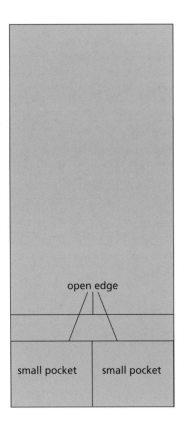

5 Attach the other two pocket sheets with tape about 10 to 12 inches (25 to 30 cm) away from the big pocket. Make sure that when you tape them into place they are not upside down when you place your caddy over the arm of your TV chair, because if you do they won't hold anything. It's that gravity thing again.

6 You'll notice that you have a long piece left over. This is the piece that gets tucked under that part of your chair where you previously found lost remotes, Cheesy Poofs, spare change and small household pets: the cushion. Placing this end under the cushion ensures that the caddy won't slip off the arm of the chair when it is loaded with the whack of items necessary for your channel-surfing enjoyment.

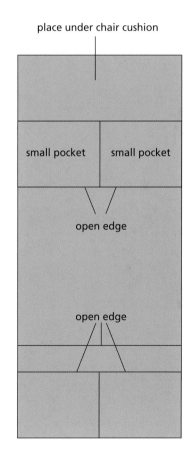

place under chair cushion

small pocket | small pocket

open edge

open edge

Pet Raingear

There are a lot of bad smells in the world — freshly fertilized fields, certain people on elevators, that unfound hard-boiled egg from last year's Easter Egg Hunt, other people's national dish — but one of the worst smells going has to be that of a wet animal. Just plain nasty. Duct-tape raingear will keep your pet dry and alleviate those pesky post-puddle-jumping pungent pet problems.

This item is by necessity a custom-made unit. How big's your pet?

1 Get your dog, cat, ferret, hamster, pot-bellied pig, Shetland pony, or whatever.

2 Measure from the base of its neck to where its tail begins. (Respect your pet's dignity at all times.)

3 For the width, decide how much of your pet you want to cover. That measurement is your width.

4 Create a sheet with these two measurements, then cut to round off the corners for enhanced comfortability.

5 Add a big strip to one end, one that is long enough to reach around your pet's neck. Then add another big strip to the sides. This should be long enough to reach underneath your pet's belly. (Allow a bit of leeway for weight gain.) To connect these straps, you may wish to purchase plastic snap-together buckles. These are available at most sporting goods stores.

6 For matching headgear, see the project "Bachelor Toilet Roll Cover." Add a brim and a chin strap. One size fits most.

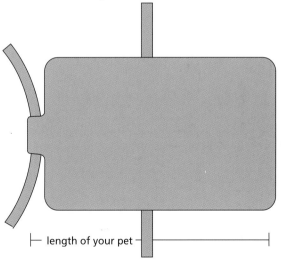

length of your pet

Bachelor's Toilet Roll Cover

We all know how important it is to have an extra roll of toilet paper in the same room as the toilet, right? Most people fear running out because, let's face it, it's embarrassing when you have to call out to someone to come to your rescue (especially when practically every household has a video camera and America's Funniest Home Videos offers so much money for footage of humiliated loved ones). Feel more comfortable with an additional roll safely sealed inside a ductigami toilet roll cover.

1 Create a sheet 14 1/2 by 4 1/4 inches (37 x 11 cm) and another sheet 6 by 6 inches (15 x 15 cm).

2 Make your sheet using 4 1/4-inch (11 cm) pieces. Trim to size and finish off the exposed edges.

3 When you get to the last piece, instead of folding it down, use it to seal the unit shut in a loop and finish off the exposed seam.

4 Now take your 6-inch (15 cm) sheet and cut out a 4 1/2-inch (11.5 cm) circle. (You can trace around a full roll of toiletpaper to make this circle.) This piece will be the top.

5 Place this circle on top of your tubular unit and use a lot of small pieces of tape to tape it into place.

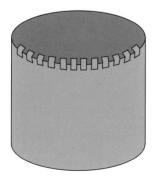

The best way to make a lot of little pieces is to lay a piece of tape on your work surface, cut it in half lengthwise, then cut the smaller pieces on an angle.

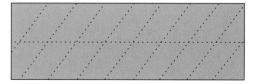

Note: The Bachelor's Toilet Roll Cover makes a wonderful hat to go with your Pet Raingear. Either keep it as is, for an exotic fez look (use red tape if you're a Shriner), or add a simple brim to create a fashionable waterproof tophat.

Tool Belt

A duct-tape tool belt? Does life get any better? This is the ultimate gift for anyone who needs a few extra pockets. It's good for handypersons, waitstaff, bingo players, you name it. The really cool thing about this tool belt is that if you don't put the tool part on it, you've still got a fine and fashionable ductigami belt.

1 Create two sheets 9 by 18 inches (23 x 46 cm) and two belt strips (measure your waist, add 2 inches (5 cm) and divide by 2 that will give you the length of each of your belt strips. You will want to buy a plastic snap-together belt buckle. These are available at most sporting goods stores.

2 Take one of your sheets and fold back 8 inches (20 cm) toward the center of the sheet. From the top of the piece you just folded over, fold 1-inch (2.5 cm) back over and close the unit so that you make a 7-inch (18 cm) pocket.

3 Repeat the above step with the other sheet.

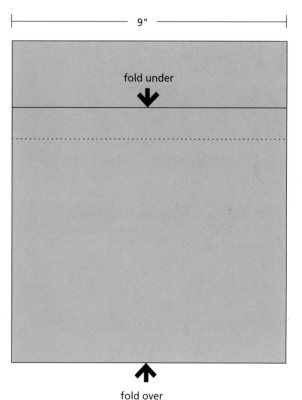

9"

fold under

fold over

4 Tape the two pockets together, front and back, and reinforce the 1-inch (2.5 cm) fold across the front with one long piece of tape.

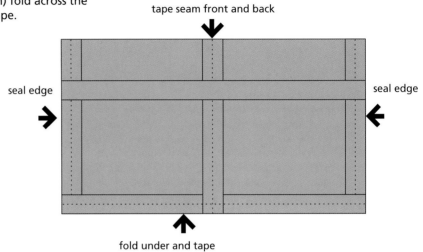

tape seam front and back

seal edge   seal edge

fold under and tape

5 Fold the remaining 3-inch (7.5 cm) piece at the top in half so that you have 1 1/2 inches (4 cm) folded over the back.

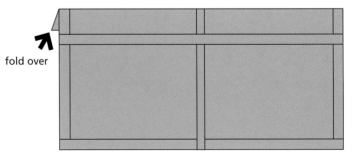

fold over

6 Now take your belt strips and tape them together to make one really big belt. Tuck it up under the fold and tape it in place. Then fold the 1 1/2-inch (4 cm) piece over the belt you just taped down. Once again, tape it down with one more really big piece of tape.

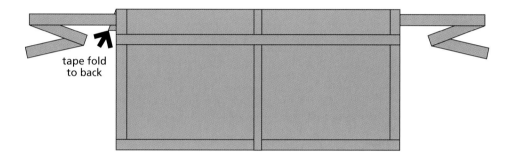

tape fold
to back

7 Attach your two plastic belt buckle pieces, adjust the belt to your waist size, and it's hammer time! (You can make one more big strip and attach it to your belt to actually hold your hammer.)

Cellular Phone Holder

Feeling kind of phoney? Got that dingling feeling? Of course, this is the Information Revolution. You must keep in touch. Every day another 16,791 people go cellular. OK, I made that number up. But if you don't have a cell phone, you soon will. And where are you going to carry it? Women who carry purses are home free, but if you're a man? I mean, are you going to stuff it in your pants pocket? "Excuse me, sir, but that big bulge in your trousers is ringing." That may have worked in a disco in the seventies, but why not send a more self-confident, more manly message. Strap on a ductigami cell phone holder. Show everyone that you're ready for anything.

This is another custom-sized unit.

1 Measure your cell phone. Triple the length of it and make a sheet that long and 2 inches (5 cm) wider than your phone. (Sounds like a math test, doesn't it? How'd you do?)

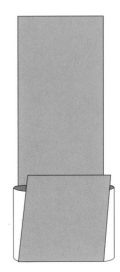

2 Fold your long piece at a third of its length. This will form a pocket when it's taped shut. Lay a piece of tape along what will be the inside of the pocket, with the sticky side down so that half of it is hanging over. Do the same on the other side.

3 Close the sides. Make sure you tape up the inside before the outside.

4 Trim the top piece to form a flap.

5 Make a belt loop and install it vertically on the back of your holder. Reinforce it.

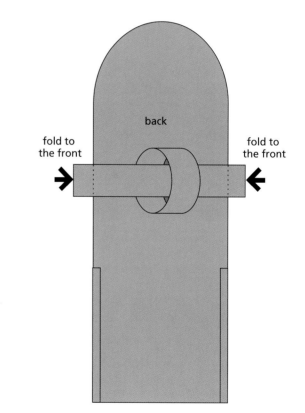

back

fold to the front

fold to the front

6 Make a little strip and install it horizontally on the front of your holder so that the flap slips underneath it.

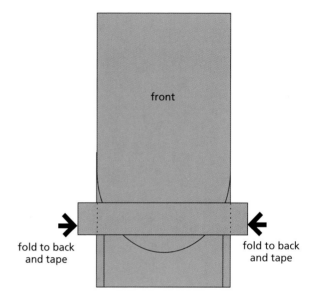

front

fold to back
and tape

fold to back
and tape

7 Trim off or cover any sticky parts. (Good general advice for all aspects of life.)

8 If necessary, cut out a small opening to accommodate your antenna.

Watchband

Remember the old Timex ads: "It takes a licking and keeps on ticking!" They beat the Hades out of those watches. Watchbands, however, seem to break at least once a year, and usually at the most inopportune moments, like when you're chipping over a water hole at the country club, shaking your fist at a used car dealer, or dancing the Macarena at the boss's daughter's wedding. Suddenly, you go strapless. All you need is a bit of duct tape and a few quick, masterful folds to create a sturdy, stylish, waterproof watchband with old-fashioned stick-to-it-iveness. Make several, in a variety of colors, for all your outfits and occasions. Watch this...

The next four steps must be done twice.

1 Measure the sides of your watchface, where your watchband attaches to your watch. This will be the width of your band.

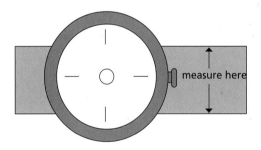

2 Measure a piece of tape 6 inches (15 cm) long. Fold over to match the proper width of your band. This is piece A.

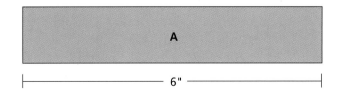

3 Measure a piece of tape 3 1/8 inches (8 cm) long. Fold over to match the proper width of your band. This is piece B. It's the same as making a little strip.

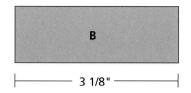

├──── 3 1/8" ────┤

4 Cut a piece tape 6 inches (15 cm) long and lay it sticky side up on your work surface. This is piece C.

5 Take piece A and place it over piece B, flush to the end of piece C.

6 Fold B in half, creating the opening for the pin that holds the band to your watch.

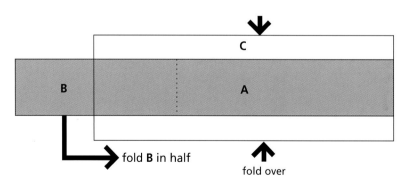

fold **B** in half

fold over

7 Complete by folding piece C over pieces A and B.

8 Create three loops. Make a test loop from a 2 1/2-inch (6 cm) piece of tape. This will make a 1-inch (2.5 cm) loop, but size the loop for your band. Make two more of the same size. Fold B to line A. Tape down C to hold in place. Now tape down D to secure.

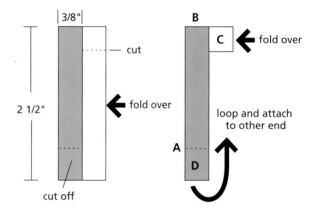

9 Place the watchband through Loop 1, then through Loop 2. Then fold it under Loop 2 and back to Loop 1. Tape the band together. This will hold Loop 2 in place. Loop 3 will hold the excess band in place.

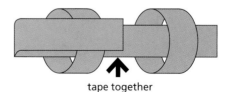

tape together

Baseball Cap

Tape me out to the ballgame.

OK, get one of those really big rolls of tape in the color of your choice. Photocopy the three pattern pieces from this book and trim them to the size of hat you want to make. (We found that if you cut the pattern pieces out of posterboard it will give you better stability when you cut your tape.) Next, put a fresh blade in your knife: the better the cuts, the better the seams.

The Panels

1 Cut three pieces of tape 8 1/4 inches (21 cm) long.

2 Take the first piece of tape (A) and lay it sticky side down on your work surface. Overlap the other pieces, piece over piece, so that your finished piece is at least 4 1/2 inches (11.5 cm) wide.

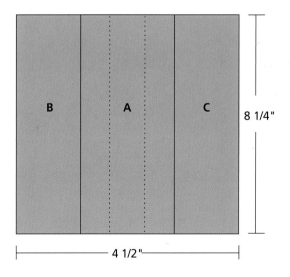

Small Pattern Piece

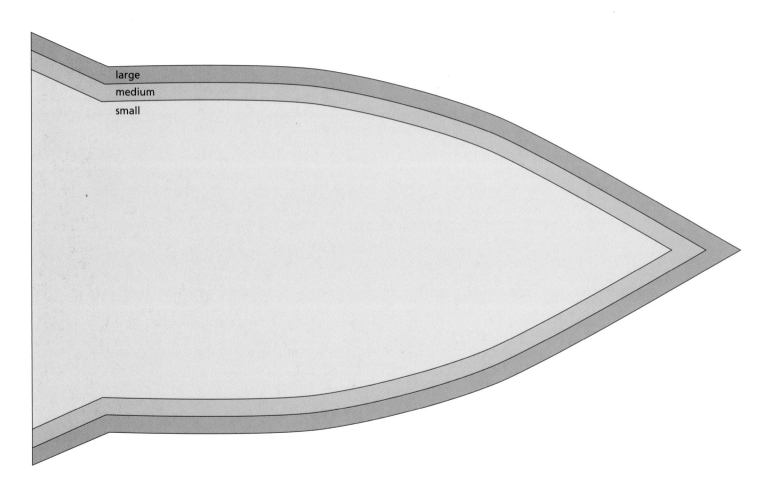

large

medium

small

Big Pattern Piece

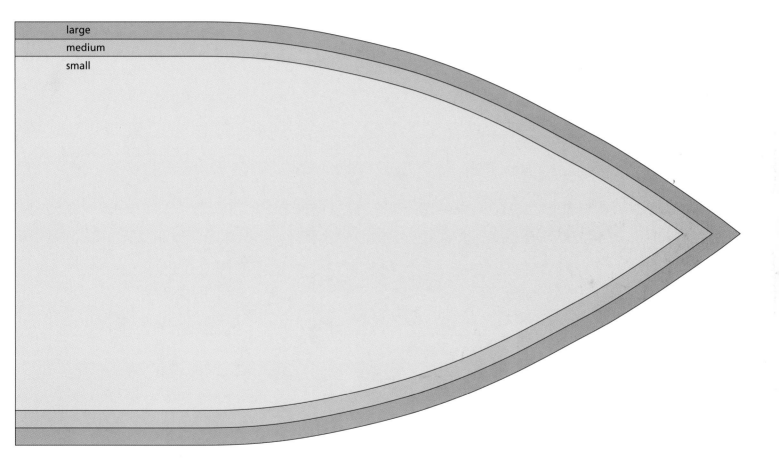

large

medium

small

Brim Pattern Piece

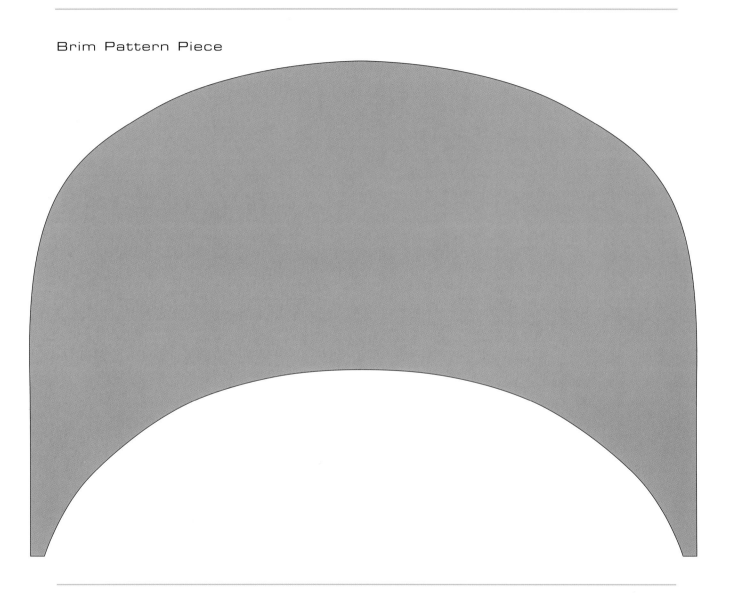

3 Take your small pattern piece and place it on the tape. Cut the tape to the pattern and remove the excess. You should end up with a piece that looks like this:

4 Grip, rip and flip so that the piece is facing you, sticky side up. Now take a piece of tape 9 7/8 inches (25 cm) long and cover the piece you just made. Put the center piece on first, then place a piece on each side so that the panel pattern is completely covered in tape.

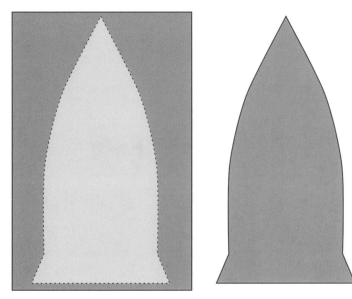

5 Take your big pattern piece and place it over the outline above. What you are trying to do is to make a piece with a 1/4-inch (1 cm) seam allowance (sticky side) around it. To do this, center the big piece as best you can, hold it in place and cut it out. You should end up with a piece that looks like the illustration at right. Hint: Line up the corners when you lay the sheet down. This will help.

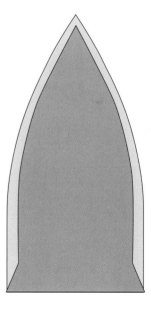

6 Repeat steps 1 through 5 two more times, so that you end up with three pieces that are exactly the same. Set these pieces aside and get ready to make the next three.

7 Do steps 1 and 2 again, but this time grip, rip and flip the entire piece over and cover the three pieces with three more pieces.

8 Now take your big pattern piece and lay it on top of this sheet. Cut out one solid piece so there aren't any sticky parts exposed. Again, you will need three of these pieces.

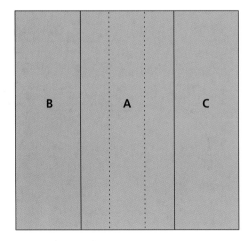

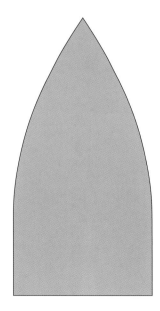

The Brim

1 Make a sheet 9 by 6 inches (23 x 15 cm).

2 Now you need to thicken this sheet up. Turn your sheet and run the next layer of tape across the grain, covering the previous layer completely. Repeat for another layer of thickening, again running across the grain. If you are using colored tape on the outside of your hat, thicken the underneath with layers of gray tape. It's less expensive. If you leave 1/4-inch (1 cm) space on top of every piece while you are thickening, you can do it all in one step.

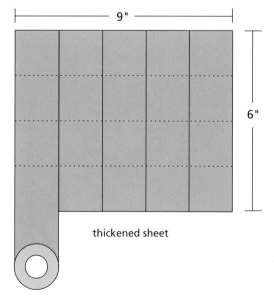

thickened sheet

3 When you are ready for your final layer (in team colors, company colors, gang colors), simply lay down strips against the grain of the previous thickening layer so that it matches the original sheet.

4 Take the pattern for your brim, place it on top of your sheet, and cut it out.

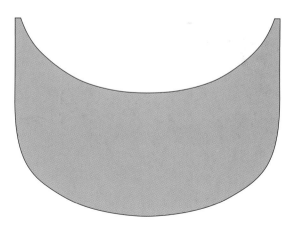

Assembly

Now you are ready to assemble your pieces. Have a cloth baseball cap nearby for reference.

1 Take one of your solid pieces and one with the 1/4-inch (1 cm) seam allowance (sticky side). Starting at the bottom, or top, shape and tape the pieces together, slowly working your way up, or down, the seam. (It doesn't matter if the top pieces overlap a bit.) While shaping your cap, try to avoid major wrinkles or creases in the tape. You should end up with two pieces taped together as in the illustration below.

2 Repeat this procedure twice more, so that you have three separate pieces when you are finished.

3 Take two of these pieces and shape and tape them together as you did in step 1.

4 Work the final piece into place one seam at a time. When you're done, you should have a cap.

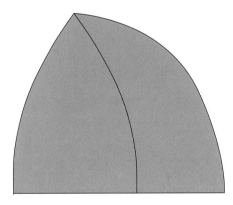

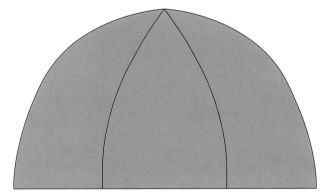

5 Now turn the cap upside-down. Seal the inside seams with tape. A lot of short pieces work better than a few long pieces. Make sure that you cover any sticky parts. Baldness should be a genetic thing, not a result of a taping accident.

6 Take your cap and fold 1-inch (2.5 cm) — more or less, according to your head size — in toward the center. Tape down the fold.

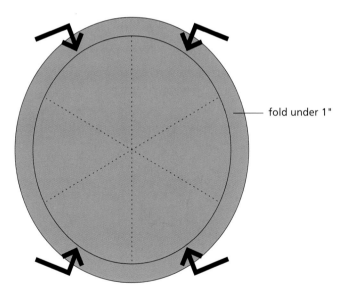

fold under 1"

7 Select the best panels to be the front of your cap. Take the brim and place it along the front. (Do this on a flat surface.) Cut a lot of small pieces of tape and begin to secure the brim to your cap along the underside of the join.

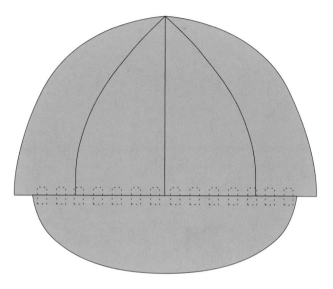

8 Once you have your cap and brim taped into place, turn the cap over and tape the top seam.

9 Cut a semi-circle out of the back of your cap. You can use the cardboard core of your duct tape roll as a guide. Make it no wider than 3 inches (8 cm) and no higher than 2 inches (5 cm).

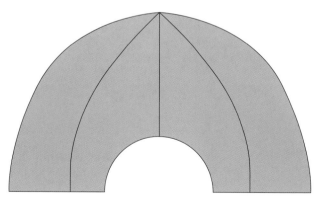

10 Finally, take a piece of tape 5 1/2 inches (14 cm) long and fold it in half lengthwise. Remember that 1-inch (2.5 cm) fold into the cap in step 6? See how it's now open on either side of your cut? Tuck one end of your strip into one side of the exposed fold. Tape it down so that it doesn't move. Now cut an opening on the other side, as illustrated, and slide the other end of your strip into it. Adjust the cap to fit your head. Tape down the rest of your strip inside the cap, and you're done. Or you can punch a few ventilation holes with a leather punch. Not a bad idea.

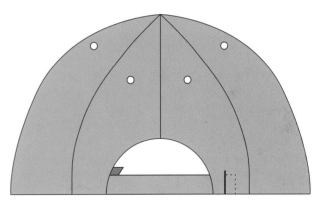

Sou'wester

Ahoy, bucko, me matey! May we never flounder, for in cod we trust. If you're more inclined to sail the high seas in search of the great white whale than you are to take in a ballgame and quaff a few pale ales, try this version.

1 Make your cap according to the instructions in the Baseball Cap project, but don't fold the 1-inch (2.5 cm) rim into the cap.

2 Create a 18 1/2-by-11-inch (47 x 28 cm) sheet and thicken it up with several layers of tape.

3 Find a bowl the same size as your cap opening and use it as a form to cut around.

4 Discard the circle that you just cut out. Cut free-hand to create a lopsided brim approximately 4 inches (10 cm) in front and 6 1/2 inches (16.5 cm) in back.

5 Tape brim into place as per instructions in the Baseball Cap project.

Now you are truly the captain of your own dinghy.

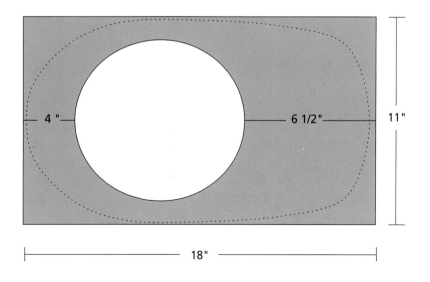

Shower Curtain / Tablecloth / Poncho

Here's a project that you can do if you have a lot of time on your hands or, come to think of it, if you're doing time. It requires a fair amount of tape, so stock up. Bribe a guard if necessary.

1 First, make eighty-one 8-by-8-inch (20 x 20 cm) sheets.

2 Lay them out nine sheets long by nine sheets wide and tape them together, front and back, to create a massive 6-by-6-foot (1.8 x 1.8 m) sheet.

3 Finish off any rough edges.

4 If you plan to use this magnificent project as a tablecloth, you're done.

5 If you plan to use this magnificent project as a shower curtain, get a leather punch and punch holes along the top to accommodate your shower curtain hooks. Then you're done.

6 If you plan to use this magnificent project as a waterproof poncho, simply cut the right size hole in the middle to accommodate your head. Warning: If you're 5 feet (1.5 m) tall, you won't need a 6-foot (1.8 m) sheet. Apply simple math and adjust the sheet size to your height. Then you're done.

The Ultimate Canine Cruiser Leash

I think I have developed the most unique duct-tape dog-walking leash of all time (who am I kidding, it's probably the only one). There's nothing worse that seeing dog-walkers clean up after their pets then carry those little plastic bags home. Stop waving to your neighbors with the bag in your hand; we all know what's in it. Here is the neat thing about the Ultimate Canine Cruiser Leash: you still have to scoop, but your pet now carries it home in the patented protein pail strategically located near the pet-end of the leash.

This one has to be built in sections and assembled while you make it. You'll need a clasp to attach to the collar. (Do not tape it your dog! They do not like it. Don't ask us how we know. All I can say is it involves scientific trial and error.)

The Leash

1 Start by making a Big Strip (see page 19) 16 inches long (40 cm), then set it aside while you make the next piece.

2 Next cut three pieces of duct tape 16 inches long (40 cm). Lay the first piece (A) sticky side up on your work area. Lay the second piece (B) sticky side down halfway up piece A. Now take the big strip piece you set aside. This is going to be the handle for the leash. Place this piece so it overlaps about 4 inches (10 cm) of the sticky side of piece A, then fold A over B to cover the big strip you have in place.

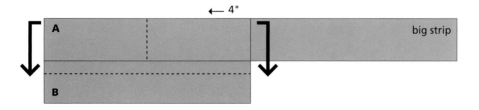

3 Again grip, rip and flip the piece over so the remaining sticky side is exposed. Place the remaining single piece that you have left, piece C, sticky side down over the exposed length of piece B. Fold your big strip piece over again so it creates a loop (the handle). Now fold C over B. You will have an open space, but don't worry, just tape it closed to reinforce your seam. (Easy, isn't it?)

4 Repeat step 2 two more times to complete the leash. Tape the last completed piece into the fold to lengthen and strengthen the leash.

5 You should end up with a piece approximately 55 inches long (140 cm) with a handle on one end. Set this piece aside. We will use it soon.

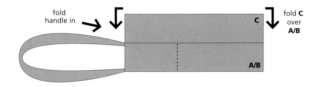

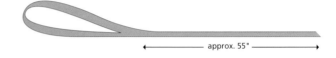

The Bag Holder

1 Make a sheet 16 inches long (40 cm) by 6 inches wide (15 cm). Square it off and lay it on your work area.

2 Now measure and make 2-inch (5 cm) cuts along both sides at these intervals: 4 inches (10 cm), 5 1/2 inches (14 cm), and 9 1/2 inches (24 cm).

3 Next, crease each cut line. After that, fold A up to B (which will be the bottom of the pouch). Now tape A to the inside of B on both sides to secure the piece in place.

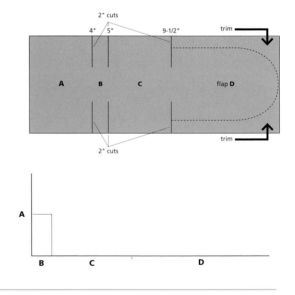

4 Fold C/D up to B and tape A/C together top to bottom, inside and out. This will also secure piece B.

5 You should have a pouch that looks like this from the side.

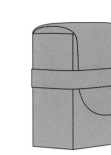

6 If you haven't done so yet, make sure that you trim piece D so that it's rounded off on the end, about 5 inches long (12 cm).

7 Make a Little Strip (see page 18) 8-10 inches long (20-25 cm). This is going to be the piece that keeps the pouch closed. Tape this strip to both sides of your pouch about halfway up. Next, fold flap piece D down and tuck it in behind the strip.

8 Take your completed pouch and cut two 1-inch (3 cm) slits into the back of it 1 inch (3 cm) from the top and then 4 inches (10 cm) from the top. Now feed the leash through these slits right up to the base of your looped handle so that the thick part of the leash is actually in the pouch. Tape it into place on the inside of the pouch, then run a piece of tape along the back to reinforce the slits and the leash, but make this piece the same width as the leash, about 1 inch (3 cm).

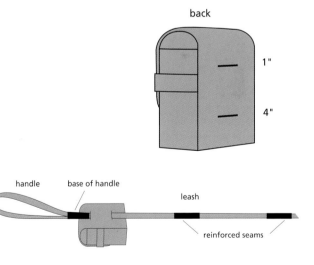

This is like building the bachelor's toilet roll cover on page 49, only with a lid.

1 Create a finished sheet 12 x 6 inches (30 x 15 cm) with trimmed edges, another sheet 4 x 4 inches (10 x 10 cm), and one more 6 3/4 x 6 3/4 inches (17 x 17 cm).

2 Take the 12 x 6-inch (30 x 15 cm) sheet and tape it together inside and out so it starts to look like a trash can or at least starts to resemble the toilet roll cover on page 49.

Now we make the lid.

3 Now take your 4 x 4-inch (10 x 10 cm) sheet and cut out a 4-inch-diameter (10 cm) circle. (I used a lid off a jar for my circle.) This piece will be the bottom. Tape it into place both inside and out.

4 With your remaining 6 3/4 x 6 3/4 -inch (17 x 17 cm) piece make a 6-inch diameter (15.5 cm) circle. (This time I used a saucer for the template circle.) Lay it on your work area.

5 Now make a little strip 12 inches long (31 cm) so that when you shape it to form a circle you should end up with a circle 4 inches (10 cm) in diameter.

6 Take your 6-inch (15.5 cm) flat circle and lay it on your work area. Center your 4-inch (10 cm) circle and slit the edges like in the diagram.

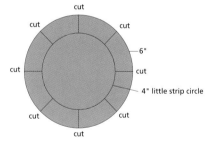

7 Fold the edges of your 6-inch (15.5 cm) circle to the 4-inch (10 cm) piece and tape it into place. You should end up with a piece that looks like this.

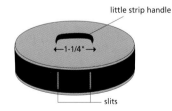

8 Now, take a 2 1/4-inch (6 cm) piece and fold it over itself to create a little handle. Make two slits in the top of the lid about 1 1/4 inches (3 cm) apart, insert the handle into the slits and tape them in place on the inside of the lid. Now you are ready to attach the lid to the leash.

8 Now, take a 2 1/4-inch (6 cm) piece and fold it over itself to create a little handle. Make two slits in the top of the lid about 1 1/4 inches (3 cm) apart, insert the handle into the slits and tape them in place on the inside of the lid. Now you are ready to attach the lid to the leash.

9 Make a little strip 5 inches (12 cm) long. Cut two slits into the side of the lid and feed the strip through, leaving a gap for the lid to slide up and down the leash. Tape it into place and slide it up the leash.

10 Take your completed pail, and on the seam (where you taped it together) cut two slits, one 1 1/2 inches (3.5 cm) from the top (make sure that the lid can close and not get in the way before you do this) and one 1 1/2 inches (3.5 cm) from the bottom. Slide the leash up through to the last reinforced joint of the leash. Tape into place again from the inside.

11 Finally, attach the clasp to your leash. Slide the leash through the opening and fold the piece back so it comes to the bottom of the pail. Tape it together and you are done. Call the dog and go for a walk.

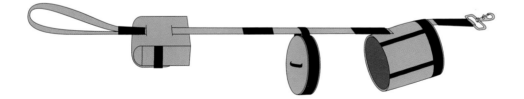

The Woven Purse

I am sure that you have enough knowledge and imagination to create a purse out of a solid sheet of tape, but here is a twist: we are going to do advanced Ductigami — the weave. (Doesn't work for hair, if anyone asks.)

1 Make fourteen 14-inch (36 cm) little strips in the color of your choice.

2 Make fourteen more 14-inch (36 cm) little strips in another colour of your choice.

3 Lay down a piece of tape 12 inches long (30 cm) on your work area. Now lay your fourteen 14-inch (36 cm) pieces side by side halfway up the 12-inch (30 cm) piece. Once completed fold the piece over to secure them.

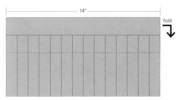

4 Now take your one of your 14-inch (36 cm) pieces and begin to slide into place at the top of your 12-inch (30 cm) piece by going over and under your 14-inch (36 cm) strips.

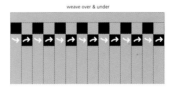

5 As you slide pieces into place, keep them as close together as you can to create a tight weave. Continue until you use all your strips and you end up with a woven sheet.

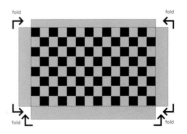

6 Now take three pieces of tape and close all open ends to complete the sheet.

Optional Liner, Credit Card Slots and Cell Phone Holder

You can cover the entire sheet with a layer of tape to act as an inside liner for the purse. Add a series of credit card slots to the inside of your purse to keep yourself organized. Add a cell phone cradle to the inside or outside of your purse so you don't have to dig for it when it rings. To do this, make two small strips based on the size of the phone, then tape them together and into place.

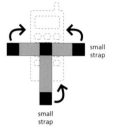

small strap

small strap

Back to the purse...

7 Take your completed woven sheet and bring the ends together so you have two open sides. Measure the open ends so you know how large of a sheet you will need to close them.

8 Once you have your measurements, make the two sheets you need to complete your purse. On one of the sheets, get a round template to create the circular bottom. (Again, I used a lid to a jar as my template.) Now cut the sheet with a round bottom halfway up the sheet. To make the final cut and make the sheet look like a giant teardrop.

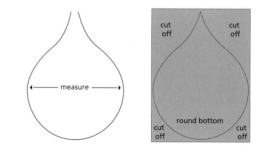

measure

cut off   cut off

round bottom

cut off   cut off

9 Once you have the piece done, put it on top of the remaining sheet, trace it and cut it so you have two identical pieces.

10 Take one of the ends and tape it into place inside and out to finish the side. Repeat on the other side to complete the purse.

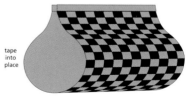

tape into place

The Shoulder Strap

11 Now make two big strips about 27 inches (69 cm) long using two pieces that match your purse. If you have trouble with strips that long, you can make three strips 18 inches long (46 cm). Once completed, tape your strips together to create one big strip 54 inches long (138 cm).

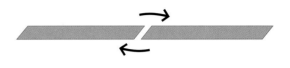

Strap Option 2

Depending on the size and the style of purse you design, you can make different handles or shoulder straps. Here's another option. Let the roll of tape hang down to whatever length you want and give the roll a spin so you form a twisted length of tape. Cut the twisted piece and set aside. On your work area, lay a piece of tape sticky side up the length of the twisted piece you created. Take the twisted piece and place it on the very bottom of the piece on your work area and roll it up to make a duct-tape cord.

12 To attach the shoulder strap to the purse, you have to cut a slit 1 1/4 inches (3 cm) from the top of the purse and another 1 1/4 inches (3 cm) from the bottom. Feed the strap through the top so that the strap is visible from the outside, and then feed it into the bottom slit and fold back up inside and tape into place. Repeat on the other side and you are done.

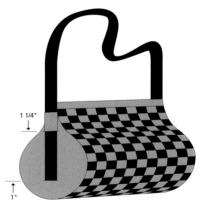

Like I said at the start, this is just one style of purse. You can make a solid-sheet or woven purse, and you can make it bigger or smaller by adjusting your measurements. You can make your sheet longer and finish it off by having a flap to close the opening. With your Ductigami knowledge and your imagination, anything is possible.

Masks

Once again, your imagination will allow you to create a variety of designs, anything from frogs to super heroes to water buffalo. Be creative! Take the lenses out of a pair of old sunglasses and use them for eyes to make one really cool alien.

1 Begin this project by making a basic hat without the brim (page 63).

2 Cut three pieces of tape 12 1/2 inches long (32 cm) and same color as your hat. Overlap them, sticky side down, by half an inch (1 cm) and make a three-piece sheet.

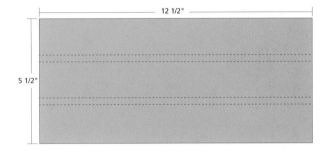

3 Grip, rip and flip the piece over and get ready to thicken it up. Do this by covering it with one layer of tape. Take pieces of tape and, starting half an inch (1 cm) from the top, lay a piece of tape down stick side to sticky side. Repeat this until the entire sheet is covered.

Before you finish, you can add eye effects to your work. Cover your thickened sheet with three pieces of another color of tape. If you want a two-colored effect, repeat this step with another color. Once you have this done, cover the sheet with three more pieces of tape the same color as the hat. (Remember that this will be the front of your mask, so if you flip it around you will not get the eye effect that you are looking for.)

4 To create the mask shape, take your template from your hat again, center it and cut out one side. Flip the template over and cut the other side.

thickened sheet

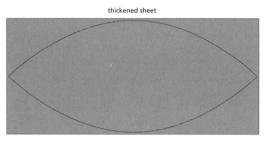

5 To create the nosepiece, take your completed mask and by holding the ends together (do not fold in half) just crease 1 1/2 inches (3.5 cm) from the bottom.

thickened sheet

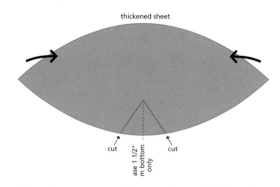

cut   cut

ase 1 1/2"
m bottom
only

6 Now we are going to do the eyes. Take your mask piece and make sure you have the right side up so you get the right eye effect. You have to draw your eye design by hand. Draw whatever kind of eyes you want right on top of the mask. (Don't worry if you make a mistake just take a damp paper towel or cloth and wipe away any errors.)

7 Creating your eye effects takes a little hand-eye co-ordination. Once you have eyes drawn, cut through the first layer and peel off the piece. Now leave a quarter inch (.5 cm) of space and follow the eye shape again. Once you are done, peel off the second layer and you should have achieved the eye effect you are looking for. Leave another quarter inch (.5 cm) of space and cut the eyehole.

cut through second layer
peel off   cut out eye

cut through first layer
peel off

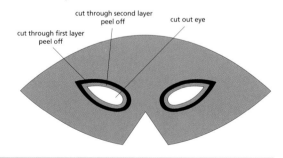

8 We are ready to attach the mask piece to the hat piece. Just as we did before we put the brim on the hat in the earlier project, select the panels that you want to be the front of the hat. Position the mask so the top of the nosepiece points to the center of the hat. Take one small piece of tape and tape it to the outside of the hat to hold it into place. Now take a lot of small pieces and begin to secure the mask to the hat.

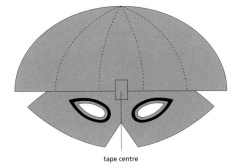

tape centre

9 Once completed, turn the hat over and tape the front of the mask to the hat.

10 To complete the mask, you have to decorate it. For this particular design, lay a piece of tape down on your work area (any size you feel comfortable with). Make even cuts along the strip so that you end up with strips about a quarter of an inch wide (.5 cm). Now decorate away. Once you feel comfortable with how it looks, guess what, you're done.

Duct Tape Suspenders

For this one, you're going to have to get some suspender hardware. You can probably find it a sewing store, or you can buy an old pair of suspenders off eBay, take the hardware and toss the rest. If you get the right suspender hardware, you can make them adjustable. If not, they'll be like these ones. You'll need three pant-clippie things. They probably have a name, but I don't know what it is. (It's not like an aglet, I know what those are. Look it up, then you'll know.) You'll also need one of those triangle suspenders things. Ask a salesclerk, use the terms "pant-clippie things" and "triangle suspenders things," and tell them that a guy named Joe sent you.

You are also going to have to get approximate body measurements for the intended wearer of these suspenders. Measure from the top of the back of the pants, up the back, over the shoulders, and down the front to the top the pants. Once you have your measurements we can get started.

1 The first piece that you have to make is going to be for the back. Make a large strip 12 inches long (30 cm). You can make it out of a solid color or a couple of colors.

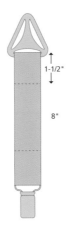

2 Once you have this done, take the triangular piece of hardware, feed the strip through the opening and fold it over so that there's 1 1/2 inches (4 cm) left over to tape down. You may have to trim some off the sides of the strip so it fits into the hardware. You want to finish this piece so that it is 8 inches long (20 cm).

3 Now we do some math. Take the total measurement that you have for your suspenders and subtract 8 inches (20 cm). Divide the remaining measurement by two to determine the length of the next big strips you are going to make. Again I suggest that you build this in pieces in order to keep crisper, cleaner strips. Once you start working with strips over 16 inches (40 cm), they can lose their shape. Once the math is done, make four large strips. Set two of them aside and join the other two together. Once that is done, attach the strip to the triangle hardware. Fold about 2 inches (5 cm) over and tape into place.

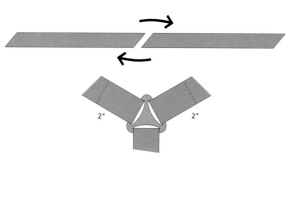

4 Repeat step 3 three more times.

5 Now we are ready to put the clasps on. If it is at all possible, put them on the person you are making them for to get a custom fit. This will give you the right measurements for the clips.

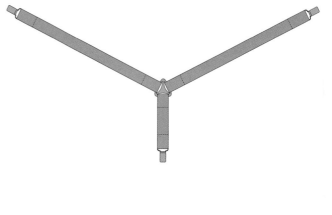

Ten Things to Do with Leftover Tape

1 Use small pieces as nameplates to label shoes, clothing, sports gear...

2 Remove a sliver.

3 Cover your heels to avoid blisters when hiking.

4 If the tabs on diapers fail or junior enjoys peeling them loose, duct tape them.

5 If you're ever in a fire, duct tape around doors and over vents to keep smoke out.

6 Hem your pants.

7 When traveling, tape your suitcase or knapsack shut to survive airport handling.

8 Temporarily replace a broken car window using duct tape and a sheet of clear plastic.

9 Remove lint from your clothing.

10 Create an emergency hinge.

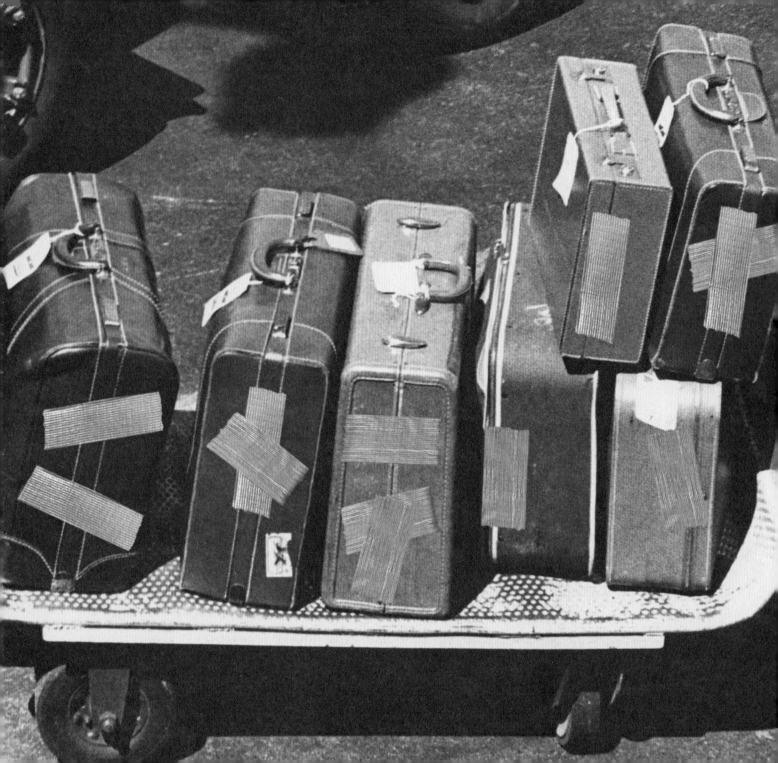